Kate Brand

Risk Taking for Chickens™

written and illustrated
by Kate Brand

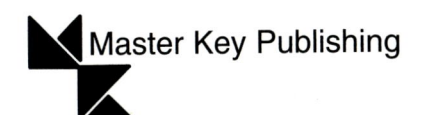

Master Key Publishing

©1997 by Kate Brand
All rights reserved.

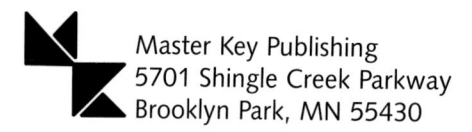

Master Key Publishing
5701 Shingle Creek Parkway
Brooklyn Park, MN 55430

Printed in the United States of America
First Printing: May 1997

ISBN 0-9657948-0-6

This book is dedicated to my heroes,
Mom and Dad,
by one of their grateful chickens!

Thank you!

To My Family...
To Marshall, for giving me courage to break out of my shell!
To Mom, my incredible model of grace and strength under pressure,
To Dad, my Motivator Man and model of positive living,
To Steve, Pat, Krs and Kim, for your generous help,
loving motivation and support.
To the Brand family, for your encouragement and heart-felt prayers.

And Friends...
To Deb Hvass, George Kline, Joe Hallett, Linda Rossi, and
Sharon Rusten, for your insights and expertise,
And to Mike Anderson and Glen Phillips; for your generosity and
quality craftsmanship that made this book possible.

Let not your heart be troubled, nor let it be afraid.[1]

Risk Taking for Chickens™

Most books and seminars on the subject of risk taking have an inherent problem. They assume that those who need them most are brave enough to open the book or walk into the seminar in the first place!

This book is written especially for those who need it most. If you have been afraid to take the next step in your personal or professional growth, or if you've been fearful of even *naming* what that next risk may be in your life, this book is for you.

Who's a Chicken?

Chicken (chi'–kən) *n.* any person who feels frightened or nervous at the prospect of taking a particular action, (i.e., risk).

Those of us whose stomachs churn at the thought of asking for a raise, whose hearts pound when confronted by that obstinate co-worker, or whose throats tighten when asked to speak in front of a group *we* have no difficulty identifying ourselves as "chickens."

Who, me? Chicken?

But it may surprise you to know that virtually everyone feels anxiety in some area of life. A top executive may feel nervous in a vulnerable relationship, a body builder may be afraid of centipedes, or a famous celebrity could be shy at parties.

In other words, you are not alone. Everyone feels fear at one time or another. And anyone can learn to overcome it ... **one risk at a time.**

Break out of your shell.
It's the only way to grow!

Breaking out of your shell

Ask any chicken. It's warm and cozy inside that egg. It would certainly be a lot more pleasant just to stay put. Especially considering the ordeal awaiting those venturesome enough to start pecking on the perimeters of their known world.

If you've ever watched an egg hatch you know what I mean. The process is painstaking. At first the egg rocks almost imperceptibly. Much later a tiny peck mark is visible on the shell. Time passes slowly. More slight movements. More tiny pecks.

Eventually a wet little chick foot spastically pushes its way through the shell. Later a pitiful, bony wing makes its escape in slow motion.

Finally, after hours of what can only be described as hard labor, the limp, soaking-wet chick lies spread-eagle. Surrounded by fragments of its former limitations, it shivers beneath a coat of sticky, matted feathers.

My heart goes out to the poor little thing as I watch the struggle. I can hardly control the impulse to reach into the nest to break the shell wide open. If I could find an outlet, I'd be tempted to plug in my blow dryer and fluff its matted feathers.

But my well-intentioned instant rescue would be a deadly mistake. Unless the chick goes through its exhausting ordeal it will not develop properly. The very act of struggling to escape helps to build the strength it will need to survive on the outside.

Every one of us finds ourselves in circumstances, lifestyles, habits, that are warm and comfortable. Even though we may admit that we have outgrown them, we are threatened to imagine leaving the security of our cozy shells.

It's cold out there. It's hard work to break out. It's a slow, often painstaking task to break old habits. And no one can crack your shell for you.

The first step is always a big one!

But every time you break a shell it opens a new world before you. Remember the last risk you took? There is no substitute for the surge of pride and confidence you feel when you know that, despite your fear, you did the right thing. You followed your dreams. You found out what you were really made of. That's the power of risk taking.

Break out of your shell. It's the only way to grow!

The Sky is Falling!

Chicken Little set the standard for chickenhood. Apparently this timid soul did not have enough real-life problems so she *invented* even more reasons to be frightened. Sound familiar?

Always dreading the worst, she imagined worse and worse worst-cases until one day she finally convinced herself that the sky was falling.

So certain was she that Chicken Little made it her personal crusade to alarm all of her barnyard friends. Life as they knew it was over. They might as well pack it in — call it quits — and resign themselves to perpetual panic.

But the sky didn't fall. It rarely does. Yet we let our imagined fears paralyze us from taking important real-life risks.

Instead of concentrating on all of the possible hazards of taking the risk, we should weigh them against the potential rewards. Do the benefits outweigh the costs? If so, this is a calculated risk that you should consider taking after asking yourself a few important questions:

Calculated Risk Taking:
Are the benefits worth the cost?

"Do I know that this is the right thing to do?"

"If I don't take this risk, will I always wonder what could have been?"

"Will I look back on my life with regret?"

The answers to these questions are often enough motivation to give even a chicken the courage to take the first uneasy step into the open.

Tail feathers shaking, the frightened chick steps bravely into the clearing. To its amazement the sky has remained intact.

Timidly, the chicken dares to take the next step. *(And the next!)*

But chickens can't fly!

We've all heard them. Exuberant speakers, teachers, preachers exhorting us to "Soar like eagles!" "Shoot for the moon!" "Dream the impossible dream!" And that's an effective technique for motivating those who are ready to hear.

But chickens can't fly! So how can we soar like eagles? What about those of us who aren't yet able to think so big? Like those who can't conceive of becoming millionaires while they desperately struggle just to pay this month's rent? And those who can't envision having a fulfilling career as they trudge to work day after day? Or what about those who can't imagine having a healthy body, when the last time they exercised was in high school gym class?

Are the chickens of the world to be excluded from achieving the ultimate dreams simply because they can't picture the outcome in one giant, mental leap? Of course not!

**If you don't have a dream —
How can your dreams come true?**

Chickens can be just as successful as anyone. The secret is to remember that tremendous dreams can start very small.

Begin by picturing what you *can* imagine for yourself. Write it down. It may be as simple as "pay the rent on time," "take a college course," or "present my proposal to the boss." Set the dream just slightly bigger than you would normally dare. (Note: At this point chickens should feel nervous. If you don't— this is not a real risk for you).

"Faith is the assurance of things hoped for, the evidence of things not seen."[2]

You'll soon discover an amazing truth about stretching your dreams. The bigger you dream ... the bigger you are *able* to dream! Once you see that you are nearing your first goal, you'll have the inner confidence to increase the next goal and the next. Instead of just paying the rent on time, you decide in addition to put aside a percentage into savings. After taking a few courses, you decide to go for a degree. Once you've presented several successful proposals to the boss, you make plans to apply for a promotion.

Risk Taking for Chickens means that you allow yourself to stretch your dreams at your own pace. When you become comfortable with a risk, it's time to stretch yourself a little further, perhaps in a different area of your life.

What if I lay an egg?

If you are a chicken worth your salt, you have been asking the question since you opened this book. What if I lay an egg? What if I fail?

You don't have to let your fear of failure stop you from taking important risks. Just remember three things:

First—you should **expect** to fail once in a while when you stretch your dreams. If you are easily reaching **every** goal, you haven't set your goals high enough! Falling short of a dream simply means that you've succeeded in stretching your vision!

If you are easily reaching all your goals ...You're not setting them high enough!

Second—you can choose to learn from your mistakes. Thomas Edison tried 50,000 "failed" experiments in his attempt to invent the storage battery. His perspective? Now "I know 50,000 things that won't work!"[3]

Learn from your mistakes, make the needed adjustments, and don't give up. Keep pecking away.

"Failure is only the opportunity to begin again more intelligently."

Henry Ford

Finally — the only failures are those who refuse to take a risk and crack their shells. Like the chicken who never breaks free, we inevitably suffocate, stifling our personal growth. Once we stop taking risks, we stop growing as human beings, (or should I say, "chickens?")

Why should the chicken cross the road?

Taking risks is uncomfortable at best. Why should we expose ourselves to the potential dangers? Why not stay safely on our own side of the road?

As long as you are stretching yourself, as long as you are taking risks, you will always have some level of fear or discomfort. That's the birthright of a chicken. But so is the incomparable satisfaction and exhilaration that come from the knowledge that *despite your feelings* you persisted in reaching another dream. You've exhibited one of the highest forms of valor; showing courage in the face of fear.

> "Courage —
> Fear that has said its prayers."
>
> Dorothy Bernard

What is the next important risk you should take in your personal or professional life?

It's time to break that shell.

Go for it!

END NOTES

[1] John 14:27

[2] Hebrews 11:1

[3] Fadiman, Clifton,
The Little, Brown Book of Anecdotes
(Boston: Little, Brown and Company, 1985).